This We Believe!

This We Believe!

MEDITATIONS ON THE APOSTLES' CREED

Timothy C. Tennent

 seedbed

Printed in the United States of America

Library of Congress Control Number: 2012955173

Paperback ISBN: 978-1-62824-012-2
Mobipocket ISBN: 978-1-62824-013-9
ePub ISBN: 978-1-62824-014-6
uPDF ISBN: 978-1-62824-015-3
Spanish Edition ISBN: 978-1-62824-016-0

Cover design by Haley Hill

Page design by Haley Hill and Kristin Goble

SEEDBED PUBLISHING
Sowing for a Great Awakening
204 N. Lexington Avenue, Wilmore, Kentucky 40390
www.seedbed.com

Dedicated to all the alumni of Asbury Theological Seminary
who day by day faithfully proclaim the gospel all over the world!

Contents

Apostles' Creed

I believe in God, the Father Almighty,
creator of heaven and earth,
I believe in Jesus Christ, His only Son, our Lord,
who was conceived by the Holy Spirit,
born of the Virgin Mary,
suffered under Pontius Pilate;
was crucified, died and was buried.
He descended to the dead.
The third day He rose again from the dead.
He ascended into heaven and sits at the right hand of God the Father
Almighty. From there, He shall come to judge the living and the dead.
I believe in the Holy Spirit,
the holy catholic Church,
the communion of saints,
the forgiveness of sins, the resurrection of the body,
and the life everlasting.

Introduction

One of the great privileges of serving as the President of Asbury Theological Seminary is traveling across the country meeting our alumni and friends. I meet hundreds of people every year. During the last two years I have seen how hungry God's people are to be taught the Word of God and to know the central teachings of the Christian faith. Throughout history the people of God have wanted clear summaries of the faith so that they could be clear on the essential truths of Christianity. Known as catechesis manuals, these were then used to develop spiritual training guides for children and new believers. The word catechesis is the same root from which we get our modern word echo. The idea is that we pass on the faith, and those who receive it would echo it, meaning that they would be able to say it back to us just as they heard it. Thus, the word catechesis simultaneously reinforces twin truths: the sacredness of the Apostolic message and a warning against those who are tempted to reconstruct the faith to conform to modern sentiments or the latest cultural wind.

These early training guides were often based on summary passages such as the Ten Commandments, the Sermon on the Mount and the Apostles'

Creed. In fact, throughout the history of the Church, Christians have recognized that there is no better summary of the Christian faith than the Apostles' Creed. For many centuries the Church has used the Apostles' Creed as a basic guide to instruct believers in the faith. Likewise, millions of parents and grandparents across the world have used the Apostles' Creed as the basic guide for instructing their children and grandchildren in the faith.

These devotionals are dedicated to exploring the Apostles' Creed, which contains the twelve most basic affirmations of the Christian faith. If you read these carefully, you will be renewed in your own faith and be better equipped to share your faith with your friends and neighbors. You will also be able to more effectively teach the faith to others.

One of the wonderful features of the Apostles' Creed is that it only uses language taken directly from the Scriptures. Therefore, I am including beneath every phrase some suggested readings. This feature enables the book to be used for personal devotion, as well as in small study groups or Sunday school, since I have received letters from many of you that my annual devotional books are being used in those settings. Also, as with my two previous devotional books, *Word Made Flesh* and *Christ the Fulfillment*, each chapter concludes with a verse written by Julie Tennent that is brought together as a full hymn at the end of the book. The hymn reminds us that all learning and growth in the Christian faith should ultimately lead us to worship.

A creed is a historic statement of Christian faith. The purpose of a creed is to give a brief, clear summary of the Christian faith. There are two creeds in the history of the Church that have been accepted by virtually all Christians everywhere. These two creeds are known as the Apostles' Creed and the Nicene Creed. The Apostle's Creed is the shorter and older of the two. The Apostles' Creed was not actually written by the twelve Apostles, but it is based on a very early version known as the Roman Symbol or Roman Creed that dates back to the second century. It is called the Apostles' Creed because it reflects the faith of the Apostles and is organized into twelve statements for each of the twelve disciples. An old tradition says that each Apostle contributed one of the affirmations of the Apostolic faith. Later, these twelve affirmations were brought together to form what we now know as the Apostles' Creed.

The twelve statements are:

1. I believe in God, the Father Almighty, creator of heaven and earth,
2. and in Jesus Christ, His only Son, our Lord,
3. who was conceived by the Holy Spirit, born of the Virgin Mary,
4. suffered under Pontius Pilate; was crucified, died and was buried.
5. He descended to the dead.
6. The third day He rose again from the dead.
7. He ascended into heaven and sits at the right hand of God the Father Almighty.
8. From there, He shall come to judge the living and the dead.

9. I believe in the Holy Spirit,

10. the holy catholic Church, the communion of saints,

11. the forgiveness of sins,

12. the resurrection of the body and the life everlasting.

Even though the Apostles didn't actually write this creed, it clearly reflects the faith of the Apostles. From ancient times, this creed (and the Roman Creed that preceded it) was used to instruct new believers before their baptism at Easter. On Easter Sunday the Church lined up the people who had gone through a period of spiritual training and would have them publicly confess their faith, just as we do today. The twelve statements were asked as questions. For example, the leader asked, "Do you believe in God the Father Almighty? Do you believe that He is the creator of the heavens and the earth?" The candidates replied, "Yes, this we believe." Then, the leader went to the next question, "Do you believe in Jesus Christ, His Only begotten Son, as your Lord?" The candidates again replied, "Yes, this we believe." This continued through all twelve affirmations, and only then were the candidates baptized as Christians.

For this reason, I have named this devotional, *This We Believe!* I want us to remember the faith of the Apostles and be renewed in our own faith as Christians. John Wesley was a master in discipling new believers. The reason we were originally called "Methodists" is because Wesley was so well known for having a particular *method* for training new believers. His method was a unique combination of small group formation, personal accountability, worship and doctrinal learning. We are grateful that John Wesley had the wisdom to include the Apostles' Creed in his own "method" for spiritual training. This is part of our heritage as Christians and as Methodists. So, let's get started!

—Timothy C. Tennent

CHAPTER ONE

I Believe in God, the Father Almighty, Creator of Heaven and Earth

Genesis 1:1, 49:25; Isaiah 44:6; John 1:1–3; Acts 14:15; Heb. 11:3

Notice that the entire Creed is structured around the Trinity: I believe in God the *Father* . . . and in *Jesus Christ*. . . . I believe in the *Holy Spirit*. Each part of the Creed begins with each person of the Trinity and says one or more phrases about who He is in Himself and then makes a statement or two on what He has done for us. It is clear that the Creed has been very carefully planned and structured for the benefit of the Church.

However, even if we did not notice the overall Trinitarian structure, we should realize that it is a Christian affirmation with the very first phrase. If the Creed had said, "I believe in God, the Almighty, creator of Heaven and Earth" it could be an Islamic creed (every Muslim could affirm that) or a Jewish creed (every Jew could affirm that). The remarkable breakthrough in the very first phrase is the affirmation that God is *Father*. The Creed opens with, "I believe in God, the *Father* Almighty." It does not simply emphasize His power, His being almighty. Rather, He is first affirmed as the *Father* Almighty. We are learning something from the beginning about the nature of God. God is a father and, therefore, He cannot be fully understood as a solitary figure, but as One who is in relationship. God has intimate communion and relationship within Himself, as Father, Son and Holy Spirit. God is eternally the Father of the Lord Jesus Christ.

This also means that God can be our heavenly father. He wants to reveal Himself to us. He wants to know us. He wants us to experience His great love! Remember how Jesus prayed in the Garden of Gethsemane, "Abba, Father . . ." This is the language of intimacy. The sound or word *dada* or *daddy* is one of the first things we ever learn to say. How fitting that when we, as the children of God, are first learning to speak as Christians, we begin with our first "Christian" words, affirming God as *father*. Affirming God as *father* is the beginning "alphabet" of Christian faith. We already know with this one word that God is a person. God is not some mercurial force at the other end of the galaxy. He is not Aristotle's "Unmoved Mover" or the vague, generic god of the philosophers. He is a personal God. He is the embodiment of holiness, love, and justice.

The Creed goes on to affirm that He is almighty, meaning He is absolutely omnipotent and holds all power. This means that nothing is too difficult for God. Notice the beauty and symmetry in confessing God as both *Father* and as *Almighty*. *Fatherhood* denotes love, tenderness, nurture and protection.

Almighty denotes power, strength, authority and might. The two beautifully complement one another. God has all power, but He exercises it in a way that reveals His love and compassion for us. In our own human experience, power and authority become abusive when they are not rooted in love and compassion. Likewise, love and compassion, however sincere, can degrade into mere sentimentality if not undergirded with power and authority. In God, these attributes find perfect balance and harmony. Today, misinformed leaders will sometimes argue that we should not call God *father* because some people have had abusive fathers. They urge us to replace the word *father* with the word *creator*. However, fatherhood speaks to the very nature of God. It is who God is. The word *creator* speaks to something God does. You cannot confuse or substitute the two. One denotes personal relationship; the other communicates function. In fact, it is even more important today to recall the greatness of God as father to help provide the positive vision of fatherhood that many are lacking.

The Creed goes on to confess that God, who is both *Father* and *Almighty*, is also the creator of the heavens and the earth. Despite the language of intimacy which opens the Creed, we nevertheless realize that we are not worshipping some tribal deity who only looks after our little group. We are being brought into relationship with the Creator of the entire cosmos! The One who spoke the universe into existence now calls us by name.

It is truly wonderful that the Apostles' Creed opens with a phrase that so clearly resonates with the opening verse of the Bible. Genesis 1:1 shatters the darkness by declaring, *"In the beginning God created the heavens and the earth."* The Apostles' Creed likewise shatters our darkness by declaring that "we believe in God the Father Almighty, creator of heaven and earth."

The Apostles' Creed is not just a doctrine to be believed; it is a truth to be celebrated. The Psalms are filled with praise to God because He is the Creator of the universe. Psalm 102:25–26 declares, *"In the beginning you laid the foundations of the earth, and the heavens are the work of your hands; they will perish, but you remain."*

Think of the frailty and transience of our lives compared with God, the Creator. The book of James says quite soberly in James 4:14, *"What is your life? You are a mist that appears for a little while and then vanishes."* James is not seeking to diminish, devalue or demoralize you or your life. However, he does want us to see ourselves in proper perspective. Compared to God's life, our whole existence is just a little passing mist. Our entire existence is entirely dependent upon God who is the source and sustainer of all life. This is the cry of David in Psalm 8:1, *"O Lord, our Lord, how majestic is your name in all the earth."* The Psalm goes on to say, *"When I consider the heavens, the work of your fingers, the moon and stars which you have set in place, what is man that you are mindful of him, or the son of man that you care for him"* (8:3–4). It is truly amazing that God has taken us, lumps of clay that we are, and has lifted us up as the stewards of His glorious creation and, ultimately, to rule and reign with Him through all eternity. For Christians, to be a steward of this glorious creation goes beyond mere environmentalism. We are called to *creation care,* which is living our entire lives in the presence of God and humbly making choices that remember that He is the Creator of the heavens and the earth.

For the Christian, one of the first steps in the faith is to accept by faith that God created the universe. Remember the words of Hebrews 11:3, *"By faith we understand that the universe was formed at God's command, so that what is seen was not made out of what was visible."*

In other words, we do not believe that matter is eternal. It had a beginning. God spoke it into existence through His powerful word. Now, even the modern cosmologists have mostly accepted the fact that matter is not eternal. Everything is traced to the Big Bang where, by their own admission, all the normal laws of physics completely break down. It seems clear that cosmologists can never really say much more than that about the origin of the cosmos. They might come to some intelligent design behind the Big Bang, but never "God the Father Almighty." That is known to us only through revelation and accepted by us through faith. *"By faith we understand that the universe was formed at God's command, so that what is seen was not made out of what is visible"* (Heb. 11:3).

This is the God of Holy Scripture. The Almighty Creator has called us to enter into a relationship with Him. My brothers and sisters, make sure your faith is set on this God who is the Lord and King of the Universe. Make certain that you are trusting in Him who spoke His Word, and the moon and stars and planets took their place in obedience to His Word. Set your faith on the Lord, the King of the Universe, who created the mountains and the streams, the birds of the sky, the beasts of the field, the great fish of the sea. Set your faith on the Lord, the King of the Universe, who created man and woman in His own image, breathed into us the breath of life, and called us into relationship with Himself and with one another. The Apostles' Creed calls us to see God's guiding hand and presence behind the entire created order. The Apostles' Creed reminds the Church up front, at the very doorway of faith, that God is not our personal chaplain or celestial valet who does our bidding. God is not someone we can control or shape in our own image. God is not just a divine vending machine, whereby we put in the right words of faith and we get out the promised blessings. The God of Christian proclamation is the God who is on the Throne. He is the Sovereign Lord. He is the eternal King. Praise God, He is also our heavenly father. It has never been summed up more eloquently than in Psalm 100:3, *"Know that the Lord is God. It is He who has made us, and not we ourselves. We are His people and the sheep of His pasture."*

I believe in God the Father, mighty yet the fount of love;
Maker of the whole creation, earth below and heav'n above.

CHAPTER TWO

I Believe in Jesus Christ, His Only Son, Our Lord

Luke 2:11; John 3:16, 20:28; Heb. 1:1–3

The Apostles' Creed should be viewed as a succinct summary of the entire Christian faith. If you were symbolically to take a boiling pot, throw all the Methodist, Baptist, Pentecostal and even Roman Catholic and Orthodox teaching into it and boil it all down to a few basic phrases that would summarize the Christian faith around which every Christian on the planet should stand in agreement, then you would end up with the Apostles' Creed. Every word has been carefully chosen. Each phrase is pregnant with meaning. Every thought is theologically rich. The Apostles' Creed serves Christians in much the same way that the Ten Commandments served the People of God in the Old Testament. There are 613 laws in the Old Testament, and the Ten Commandments are the summarizing essence of the whole. Later, Jesus further summarized the Law down to only two: Love God with all your heart, mind, soul and strength and love your neighbor as yourself (Mark 12:28–34). Both are ancient summaries of something that is much bigger and far more complex. Christians believe and practice many things that are not found in the Apostles' Creed or in the Ten Commandments. However, these great summary statements call us back to our core identity.

Today's devotional reflects on the phrase, *"and in Jesus Christ, His only Son, our Lord."* This is the second phrase of the Apostles' Creed. This phrase gets to the heart of who Jesus Christ is, apart from what He has done for us. Jesus is the central figure in the Christian faith. Of the twelve affirmations of the Apostles' Creed, six of them are about Jesus Christ. You cannot be a proper Christian without a clear understanding of who Jesus Christ is. This is the heartbeat of the New Testament revelation. All of the major heresies throughout the history of the Church—from the Gnostics and Arians of the ancient Church to the modern day Jehovah Witnesses and Mormons—end up unleashing forces that are destructive to the Christian faith because they set themselves against the unique supremacy of Jesus Christ. The Arians and modern day Jehovah Witnesses teach that Jesus is a created being who doesn't share in God's eternality. Mormons deny the uniqueness of God, teaching that all of us can become gods. Gnostics did not believe that God would ever condescend to enter human flesh. Even modern Protestant liberals want to portray Jesus as just a great moral example, or someone on par with other great religious leaders, such as Muhammad or Buddha.

In contrast, the Scriptures declare the following about Jesus Christ: "*In the past God spoke to our forefathers through the prophets at many times and in various ways, but in these last days He has spoken to us by His Son*" (Heb. 1:1).

According to the Scriptures, the entire Old Testament was pointing to and preparing for the coming of our Lord Jesus Christ. In the past, there were many prophets and priests and means through which God the Father revealed Himself, but now it has all culminated in the revelation of His Son, our Lord Jesus Christ. Jesus fulfills the Old Testament Law. He fulfills the Jewish Priesthood. He fulfills the sacrificial system. Jesus fully embodies God's righteousness. All the prophets point to Jesus Christ. Indeed, all revelation points to Jesus Christ because He is uniquely God's "only Son." He is the second person of the Trinity: Father, Son and Holy Spirit. Today, there is a call by some to move away from the traditional language of the Trinity—Father, Son and Holy Spirit—and move toward gender neutral language, such as Creator, Redeemer, and Sanctifier. There are two main reasons why this suggestion has been wisely rejected by the Church. First, the language of "Father, Son, and Holy Spirit" is language taken directly from Scripture which reveals the relational nature of God. If we lose the relational language that lies at the heart of the Church's language about the Triune God, then we are left only with the abstract god of the philosophers or Allah (the God of Islam), who has no interest in revealing himself, only declaring his will. Non-relational language should not be used for the God of Scripture.

Second, words such as *"creator," "redeemer"* and *"sanctifier"* are wonderful words, but they declare what God has *done*, not who He *is*. The phrases "God the Father" and "Jesus Christ, His only Son" are in the Creed because they confess who God is, not just what He has done. The Apostles' Creed and the later Nicene Creed always begin by confessing who God is before they declare what He has done. We should rejoice in and affirm the full beauty and power of the phrase "His only Son."

The final word in this phrase of the Apostles' Creed asserts that Jesus is "our Lord." This is an affirmation of the deity of Jesus Christ. Occasionally, you will hear modern day skeptics say that the Scriptures never explicitly call Jesus *God;* therefore the Church should not proclaim the full deity of Jesus Christ. Our response to this charge is to first point out that there are five times in the New Testament where Jesus is actually called *God* (Heb. 1:8; Rom. 9:5; Titus 2:13; 2 Peter 1:1, John 20:28). However, the deity of Christ is not determined by simply these passages in the New Testament that call Him *God* or the dozens which call Him *Lord*. Instead, the deity of Christ is affirmed not only by divine *titles*, but also through divine *actions* and divine *prerogatives*. When Jesus raises Lazarus from the dead and declares, *"I am the Resurrection and the Life"* (John 11:25), it is an assertion of His deity even though the word "God" is not specifically used. When Jesus forgives sins, even His opponents remark (Mark 2:7), *"Who can forgive sins but God alone?"* When Jesus receives worship, it is a powerful pointer to His deity (Matt. 2:11, 14:33, 28:9, 17; Luke 24:52; John 9:38; Heb. 1:6), even if the word *"God"* or *"Lord"* is not explicitly used. Jesus' declaration that He was with the Father before the foundation of the world (John 17:24), that He had a special prerogative to judge the entire world (John 5:22, 27) and that He has all authority and power (Matt. 28:19) clearly indicate His deity. Colossians 1:16 declares, *"For by Him (Jesus Christ) all things were created in Heaven and on earth, visible and invisible, whether thrones or powers or rulers or authorities; all things were created by Him and for Him."* Note that this text not only declares that the world was created *by* Him, but that all of creation was *for* Him, i.e. for the manifestation of His divine glory!

Hebrews 1:3 says, *"The Son is the radiance of God's glory and the exact representation of His being, sustaining all things by His powerful word."* The picture here is that of the sun shining its radiant glory, light, and life to the earth. If the sun at the center of our solar system were to stop shining, in eight minutes the earth would be in darkness, and within a few days we would all rapidly plunge into a deep freeze of death. The sun daily radiates warmth, light and life-sustaining energy to the entire planet. In the same way, Hebrews declares that Jesus Christ is the radiance of God's glory. Through Jesus Christ, God radiates His glory and presence to the earth. Jesus is the imprint of the Father. He fully bears the glory and nature of the Father. He is the exact representation of His being. This is why Colossians 1:16 declares, *"For God the Father was pleased to have all His fullness dwell in [Christ] Him,"* and Colossians 2:9 asserts, *"For in Christ all the fullness of the Deity dwells in bodily form."* Jesus is fully God, the radiance of God's glory, the exact representation of His being who created the world and then, through the incarnation, entered the world of His creation to redeem us. This is what the Apostles' Creed affirms when it says, "and in Jesus Christ, His only Son, our Lord." He is both the eternal Son of God and, through the incarnation, He has become our Lord and our Savior.

I believe in Jesus Christ, His only Son before all time;
All authority is His, our Lord and Savior, Word divine.

CHAPTER THREE

Who was Conceived by the Holy Spirit, Born of the Virgin Mary

Luke 1:26–27, 35

From all eternity the Son is in the Father and the Father is one with Son. Yet, in the fullness of time, God sent forth His Son (Gal. 4:4), the expression and extension of His radiance, Word, and glory, into the world. This is the great mystery of the incarnation. The Apostles' Creed declares, "He was conceived by the Holy Spirit, born of the Virgin Mary." The eternal God stepped off His throne and clothed Himself in human flesh and stepped into our history. Because of the Trinity, God the Father continues to govern and rule the universe and, yet, God the Son is born into the world as the Word made Flesh in Jesus Christ. The very One who had created the world is now born into the world of His creation. This mystery leads us to stand in awe and to worship. Remember the words of Charles Wesley in reflecting on the mystery of this great truth:

"Christ, by highest Heaven adored; Christ the everlasting Lord! Late in time behold Him come, offspring of the virgin's womb. Veiled in flesh the Godhead see, hail the incarnate deity; pleased as man with men to dwell, Jesus our Emmanuel."

God the Son is born into the world, and although He is the eternal God, He takes on human flesh and becomes a man. Remember, John's gospel declares, *"The Word became flesh and dwelt among us"* (John 1:14). Now, as the incarnate One, He is fully God and fully man. He is not a mixture of the two. Jesus Christ is not half God and half man. He is *fully* God and *fully* man, yet united into one person. This is such an amazing mystery that words can hardly describe it. Indeed, some of God's attributes are so incompatible with humanity that God the Son had to temporarily suspend the exercise of some of His attributes (such as omnipresence, i.e. being all places at the same time). Jesus was only in one place at a time. Jesus taking human form is such an amazing mystery that the Apostle Paul, when describing Jesus in the book of Philippians, breaks out in a hymn of praise:

Who being in very nature God,
Did not consider equality with God something to be grasped,
But emptied Himself, taking the very nature of a servant,
Being made in human likeness.
And being found in appearance as a man, He humbled Himself (Phil. 2:5–8).

One of the great novels in English literature is Mark Twain's *The Prince and the Pauper*. The story depicts the life of the son of King Henry VIII who was heir to the throne of England. He met a poor, ragged pauper boy on the streets of East London, and they realized that they shared a remarkable resemblance. They agreed to trade clothes. The Prince, the future King of England and heir to the throne, went out into the streets of London dressed as the pauper and nobody recognized him. People spat on him and pushed him aside, little knowing that he was the heir to the throne.

Likewise, the eternal Son of God clothed Himself in our humanity and walked among us and most did not recognize Him. John 1:10, 12 says, *"He was in the world, and though the world was made through Him, the world did not recognize Him . . . yet to all who received Him, to those who believed in His name, He gave the right to become children of God."*

God the Son was conceived by the Holy Spirit and clothed in flesh in the womb of Mary, one of God's humble servants. We should always honor Mary as a wonderful example of obedience and submission to God. Her humility and obedience are recalled by virtue of her name appearing in the Creed. The Creed only references two people who lived in the first century, Mary and Pontius Pilate. Mary is, therefore, the only person of faith noted in the Creed. In the next chapter, I will say more about why Pontius Pilate's name is mentioned. However, Mary's name appears to remind us that obedience and submission to God are not things that occur only in the rarified air of the heavenly counsels where the Son of God agrees to become incarnate and suffer on behalf of a fallen human race. Rather, Jesus' obedience to the Father is mirrored by the obedience of a young, Jewish peasant girl on earth. Indeed, in the wonderful providence of God, the great themes of salvation and redemption do not unfold on the earth apart from many small acts of obedience and faithfulness by people like you and me. God does take the initiative to redeem the world. However, He also chooses to do it with the cooperation and involvement of ordinary people. It is truly an awesome point of reflection that the obedience and humility of the Son of God are placed side by side with the obedience and humility of Mary.

The Apostles' Creed does not merely state that Jesus was born to Mary, but born of the *virgin* Mary and *"conceived by the Holy Spirit."* Why was it necessary for Jesus to be born from a virgin and to be conceived, not by a man, but by the Holy Spirit? Why was this so important that it was included in the Apostles' Creed, which by all accounts, represents only the central core of the Christian faith? The answer is rooted in the necessity that Jesus be without sin. According to Scripture, there are two ways in which we are declared sinners. First, we are declared sinners, quite obviously, because we have all committed sinful acts through our thoughts, words and deeds. We have sinned through what we have done and what we have left undone. However, second, we are also declared sinners because we inherit the guilt of Adam's sin in the Garden of Eden. When Adam rebelled against God in the Garden, he was not just acting on his own. He was the *representative* man, acting on behalf of the whole human race. When Adam eats, we are all brought into this rebellion. Adam had a real choice to obey or to disobey. However, since he disobeyed, we are all swept into the rebellion and are born with a sinful nature. This means that we have a tendency toward sin and a physical and spiritual inertia driving us toward death. Every day, we confirm by our choices that this is indeed our natural state. We are constantly battling this proclivity to sin and self-will. As Paul puts it, we are now all *"dead in our transgressions"* (Eph. 2:1–5). Thus, for Jesus to be the spotless "Lamb of God" without sin, He has to not only live a sinless life, but also be born without a sin nature or any of the stain of Adam's guilt. The virgin birth and Holy Spirit conception solves this dilemma by, on the one hand, assuring that He is fully human by coming forth from the womb in the same way as all of us have. Yet, on the other hand, by being conceived by the power of the Holy Spirit, Jesus is not tainted by Adam's sin and, therefore, can come into the world as the Second Adam. He can recreate Adam's choices, choosing obedience where the first Adam chose to rebel.

This phrase of the Apostles' Creed is confessing the great mystery of the incarnation. One way to illustrate this mystery is found in Trafalgar Square in London. The central monument in that great square is Nelson's Column. Horatio Nelson is, of course, the great eighteenth-century naval hero in British history. In 1805, he defeated both the French and Spanish fleets at Trafalgar, which is still considered to be one of the greatest naval victories in the history of the world. However, he was fatally wounded in the battle and died on ship soon after he heard the news of the victory. To honor him, the

British built Trafalgar Square and erected a huge column with his statue on top. However, the column and statue is so high (169 feet, 3 inches!), a visitor to the square cannot actually get a glimpse of Nelson. Visitors to Trafalgar square have no idea what he looks like. So, the British have an exact replica, a duplicate of Nelson's image, at the ground level so that visitors can look him in the eye and see him face to face. This is a picture of the incarnation. The Triune God is so high and exalted we couldn't know Him or see Him. However, in the incarnation, God came down in Jesus Christ so that we could behold Him face to face and see His glory. In that poignant moment in the Upper Room, Jesus tells His disciples just prior to His passion that He must leave them and return to His Father. He says to them in John 14:6, "*I am the Way and the Truth and the Life; no one comes to the Father except through Me.*" Philip speaks up and says, "*Lord, show us the Father.*" Jesus says, "*If you have seen me, you have seen the Father.*" He is the imprint or exact replica of the Father in human flesh. The word "*incarnation*" means literally *in the flesh*. In Jesus, we see God *in the flesh*. This is the glorious mystery and truth confessed by the Apostles' Creed: "We believe in Jesus Christ, His only Son, our Lord, who was conceived by the Holy Spirit and born of the Virgin Mary."

> *He stepped into time and hist'ry, by the Spirit was conceived;*
> *Born in flesh of Virgin Mary, humble servant who believed.*

CHAPTER FOUR

He Suffered Under Pontius Pilate; was Crucified, Died and was Buried

Luke 23:23–35; John 19:18–20; Acts 4:10; 1 Cor. 15:3–4; Heb. 2:5–18

Six of the twelve affirmations of the Apostles' Creed focus on Jesus Christ. This is, in itself, a remarkable testimony to the centrality of Jesus Christ in the earliest teaching and preaching of the Apostles. They recognized that in Jesus Christ something entirely unique had occurred in the human race. The whole of Jesus' life, ministry, work and passion all point to this remarkable truth: In Jesus Christ, God Himself miraculously stepped into our world and walked among us. The Creed provides the two bookends, as it were, to this amazing mystery: His miraculous birth and His miraculous death. The Creed first speaks of His miraculous birth. Then the Creed jumps to the miraculous culmination of His life in His crucifixion: "He suffered under Pontius Pilate, was crucified, died and was buried." We should not take this swift move from

Christ's birth to His death as any indication whatsoever that His teaching, ethical life, miracles or anything else in His public ministry were not important to the early Church. Rather, we are reminded that the Apostles' Creed merely frames the great events of God in Jesus Christ, realizing that the Church has much more to proclaim, teach and preach than the Apostles' Creed. The Church's message is much *more* than the Apostles' Creed. The point of the Creed is to remind us, however, that the Church's message can never be *less* than the Creed. This is the irreducible heart of the Christian message.

At the heart of the Christian message is a proclamation of the centrality of Jesus' death. So, let's try to answer the question: Why did Jesus have to die? To answer this question probes the very depths of the Christian message. Indeed, the cross is the central symbol of Christianity. In isolation from the Christian message, a cross is nothing more than a symbol of suffering, shame, torture, punishment and death. For the Christian, the cross symbolizes the great intersection of God's holiness and God's grace at Christ's crucifixion. God's holiness demanded that sins be paid for; God's grace provided the payment for us! Muslims say it is blasphemous to even think about God coming to earth or dying—to them it is just one big, shocking blasphemy. For Christians, Christ's death is the source of our greatest celebration and hymns. Charles Wesley wrote:

> *"He left His father's throne above, so free, so infinite His grace; emptied Himself of all but love and bled for Adam's helpless race; Tis' mercy all, immense and*

free, for O my God it found out me—Amazing love, how can it be, that Thou my God shouldst die for me!"

Robert Lowry also wrote:

"On the mount of crucifixion fountains opened deep and wide; from the floodgates of God's mercy flowed a vast and gracious tide. Grace and love like mighty rivers poured incessant from above; Heaven's peace and perfect justice kissed a guilty world in love."

In Hebrews 2:5–18 we have one of the best answers to this question. In this passage the writer seeks to answer the questions: If Jesus is the Lord of the universe, then why was He subjected to such horrific suffering? If Jesus really is God incarnate, the radiance of God's glory, the exact representation of His being who upholds all things by the Word of His power, then why did God allow Himself to be put through such a painful ordeal? If Jesus really is superior to the angels, why do we see Him in such a humiliated state on the cross? To put the whole thing rather bluntly, why did Jesus have to die? That is the key question. Jesus had to die upon the cross for three reasons.

First, He died so that He might taste death for everyone. Hebrews 2:9 says, *"He suffered death, so that by the grace of God, He might taste death for everyone."*

Jesus taking our place is one of the most powerful truths of the Christian faith and the cross of Christ. The formal name for it is the *substitutionary atonement*. In a nutshell, Christ died on the cross as a substitute for you and for me. He took our place. We are sinners and, therefore, have willfully joined in Satan's rebellion against God. In God's justice He has declared us guilty and the punishment is death. Romans 6:23 declares that *"the wages of sin is death."* In other words, we have been sentenced to death for our sins. We are brought in cuffs out of the courtroom and are led to the execution chamber. We are strapped in, prepared to die. Suddenly, we get word that the very judge who declared us guilty has allowed His Son to die in our place as a substitute. Paul says in 1 Corinthians 15:3, *"For what I received I passed on to you as of first importance, that Christ Jesus died for our sins, according to the Scriptures, and that He was buried."* This is the scriptural source of the very language of the Creed. Every phrase of the Apostles' Creed comes directly out of Scripture. Jesus died for our sins—as a substitute. Jesus died so that we do not have to taste spiritual death.

Second, He died to express solidarity with the human race, making us all one family (Heb. 2:10–13).

The whole incarnation, from His birth to His death, reflects His solidarity with the human race. We are learning righteousness and obedience through the whole of His life. When Jesus was born, the very act of passing through the birth canal and being born into this world with trauma and pain is an expression of amazing solidarity. It is a mystery we can't fully comprehend. Later, as an adult He stood in the Jordan River and presented Himself to John the Baptist for baptism. John objects and says, "I need to be baptized by you." But Jesus answered him and said, *"Let it be so, it is necessary to fulfill all righteousness"* (Matt. 3:15). Jesus didn't need to be baptized because of any sin in His life, but His mission called for Him to stand in solidarity with us and show us how to live in righteousness. All of this culminates in the death of Christ, which is the greatest act of solidarity with the human race—actually identifying not just with our human experience—hunger and tears—but with our sin and our death. *"The Father made Him who knew no sin to be sin on our behalf, that we might become the righteousness of God"* (2 Cor. 5:21). Then, Hebrews 2:9 goes on to say, *"But we see Him who for a little while was made lower than the angels, namely Jesus, crowned with glory and honor because of the suffering of death, so that by the grace of God He might taste death for everyone."*

In this context we have to understand what is meant when the very next verse (Heb. 2:10) says that the Father should *"make the author of their salvation perfect through suffering."* Christ embodies perfect righteousness, perfect obedience. When the Bible says that Jesus is "made perfect" through suffering, it does not mean that He was not perfect or holy. In the ancient world they distinguished between untested obedience and tested obedience, between untested strength and tested strength. For example, if someone were a very strong and mighty man with a great, big shield, a huge, sharp sword, tremendous biceps and arm length and everything else imaginable, you might conclude, "There is a mighty warrior, strong and mighty. I don't want to get into a scuffle with him." Now, the ancients would say, in effect, maybe so, maybe not. You never know for sure if someone is a mighty warrior until he has been tested in actual battle. It is like looking at a beautiful car before you actually give it a test drive. The proof is in the driving. For a warrior, the proof was in the fighting. If he fought and proved that he was indeed all that he claimed to be, then his claims were perfected or confirmed. This is reflected in 1 Kings 20:11 where the king of Israel said to Ben-Hadad, *"Let not him who straps on his armor boast as he who takes it off."* Similar proverbs occur throughout Jewish literature.

Jesus, the eternal Son of God, was perfect and without sin, but He had never been tempted. He had never been subject to suffering. Yet, in the incarnation Jesus experienced temptation, suffering and all kinds of trials. For this reason, the writer declares, *"He has been made perfect through suffering"* (Heb. 2:10). Through the incarnation His perfection was *confirmed*, not just in theory in the heavens, but in practicality through His facing battles on our behalf.

In *Mere Christianity*, C. S. Lewis makes the helpful point that only someone who has resisted temptation knows the full power of temptation. If you regularly and even quickly give in to temptation, then you don't actually know its full power. Only someone who has resisted temptation to the very end and never given in truly understands the power of temptation. From that perspective, only Jesus knows the true power of temptation since only Jesus has actually resisted temptation to the end and never succumbed to it (*Mere Christianity*, New York, MacMillan Press, 125).

Third, He died to destroy him who holds the power of death, i.e. the devil (Heb. 2:14).

The modern world likes to downplay any notion of sin, evil or the devil. One of the few benefits of September 11, 2001 was that it sent people scrambling to recover some of our lost moral vocabulary. We weren't able to re-claim the words *"sin"* and *"devil,"* but at least we got the word *"evil"* back. Speaking frankly, our world will never recover words such as *"sin"* and *"Satan"* without the revelation of the Bible. The Scripture reminds us that a personality exists behind the rebellion to which we have united ourselves. That personality is known as Satan or the devil.

First Peter 5:8 says, *"Your enemy the devil prowls around like a roaring lion, seeking someone to devour."* Evil is not just some vague mist that blows across our world or the collective influence of societal structures. Evil is embodied, and the rule of evil is extended and advanced through real personalities. Satan oversees a vast network of demonic powers; Satan is the head of the diabolical kingdom. Satan is served by some major dark forces known in Scripture as principalities and powers. This is why the Apostle Paul says, *"We wrestle not with flesh and blood, but with principalities and powers and rulers of this dark world and against the spiritual forces of evil in the heavenly realms"* (Eph. 6:12).

We see in this text that the victory of Christ was personal, not impersonal. Christ personally confronted the powers of this dark world. Satan had tempted Adam and Eve in the Garden, unleashing a rebellion in the human race. Satan is the head of the rebellion. Jesus came not just to defeat the idea of evil or even subdue our capacity to sin in our own lives, but to defeat and to destroy Satan. This battle took place on the stage of human history. This is why the Apostles' Creed says, "He suffered *under Pontius Pilate.*" Pilate is a defined, known figure in human history who made specific choices that unwittingly lent his support to Satanic principalities and powers arrayed in opposition to God and His people. Jesus did not suffer in some ephemeral way or on some supernatural plane. Jesus suffered in real history. He was delivered over to crucifixion by the instrumentality of a whole range of human decisions to participate in evil, including religious and political leaders such as Pontius Pilate. Just as Mary's presence in the Creed calls to mind the power of human choices to obey, the inclusion of Pilate in the Creed reminds us of the awesome consequences when we make decisions opposing God's will. This is not a movie. This is not merely a projection of human aspirations about what a loving, self-sacrificing God might be like. The Creed is rooted in real historical events whereby God interacts on the stage of human history, and people like you and me make real choices to obey or disobey. What an amazing truth! Just think of how this empowers and enlivens every day of our lives.

Jesus suffered under Pilate, and was cruelly crucified;
Entered death which was our sentence, ours the sin for which He died.

CHAPTER FIVE

He Descended to the Dead

Luke 23:43; Eph. 4:4, 6:12; 1 Peter 3:18–20

The phrase *"He descended to the dead"* or, in some versions, "He descended into hell" has troubled some modern Christians who have not taken time to study the history or meaning of this phrase. Several United Methodist hymnals actually omitted this phrase from the Creed, though in the current *United Methodist Hymnal* the traditional, ecumenical version is given alongside of the modern, amended one (881, 882). However, every word and phrase of the Creed was carefully chosen. No phrases can be jettisoned as unnecessary. More importantly, no single denomination or group has the authority to change or amend a creed because the historic, ecumenical creeds (Apostles' and Nicene) belong to the entire Church throughout the world and back through time. Denominations can write and adopt, should they choose, particular statements of faith which affirm beliefs or practices specific to a denomination. But there is an important distinction between a creed and a statement of faith. On the one hand, a creed is an historic statement that is affirmed by Christians all across time and applies to all churches everywhere. On the other hand, a statement of faith might include more specific views regarding baptism, speaking in tongues, church government, rapture and so forth, which would not necessarily be shared by churches all over the world.

The phrase, *"He descended to the dead"* refers to the period between the death of Christ and His resurrection. The early Church did not understand the death of Christ on Friday and His resurrection on Sunday as two separate events (as they are often understood and thought of by modern Christians). Rather, they understood the entire drama to unfold as one continuous event. For most Christians, Good Friday and Easter Sunday have great meaning, but we are not so sure how these events are connected by Holy Saturday. The biblical understanding, however, is that after Jesus died upon the cross for our sins, He descended to the place of the dead, and important, redemptive events unfolded throughout the time subsequent to His death, culminating in His resurrection on Sunday morning.

According to Scripture, there are three key events which took place in Sheol, the Jewish name for the place of the dead.

First, Jesus proclaimed the gospel to people throughout time who are awaiting their full deliverance. Sheol is a very general term and is the designation both for the place of torment as well as for paradise. Jesus descended into Sheol, or the place of the dead. Sometimes the Creed translates this phrase as "He descended into hell" or, more generally, "He descended to the dead." This latter, more general, translation is probably preferred because the word *"hell"* is associated only with the place of torment for the unbelieving dead. However, Sheol contained both the righteous and the wicked. There in the place of the dead, Jesus preached the gospel. 1 Peter 3:18–20 describes this descent and proclamation by Jesus Christ on Holy Saturday between His death and His resurrection:

For Christ died for sins once for all, the righteous for the unrighteous, to bring you to God. He was put to death in the body but made alive by the Spirit, through whom also He went and preached to the spirits in prison who disobeyed long ago when God waited patiently in the days of Noah while the ark was being built.

After the crucifixion Jesus descended to the place of the dead and preached. The text makes specific reference to those dead who lived prior to the flood, but the Church has generally understood this as indicating how Jesus preached to people all throughout time, not just those who had recently died. It is a way of saying "even the ancient people" heard this proclamation.

In later Christian tradition (though not mentioned in the Scriptures) a great emphasis was placed on Jesus coming into Hades as the second Adam and rescuing the first Adam as a way of symbolically demonstrating the power of Jesus' redemption of the human race and the decisiveness of His victory over Satan. St. Ephrem the Syrian (306–373) was one of the great hymn writers of the early Church, writing hundreds of Christian hymns. Several of his hymns celebrate Jesus' descent into hell and His confrontation with Satan. One of Ephrem's hymns says that Satan refused to release Adam because he had not been baptized, nor was he covered by the shed blood of Jesus. At that moment back on earth, the soldier who wanted to prove that Jesus was truly dead stuck a spear into His side and *"at once there came out blood and water"* (John 19:34). The blood and water that poured out, sings Ephrem, baptized Adam and the blood covered Adam's sins. This is, of course, not intended to be any literal description of what happened or even a proper interpretation of the water and blood that came from Jesus' side. Rather, Ephrem is drawing on the rich symbolism of this event to make the larger, and accurate, theological point that Jesus' death had a cosmic reach that affected the entire human race.

Second, the descent to the dead expresses the full victory of Jesus Christ over Satan and all the principalities and powers of evil. This is known in Christian tradition as the "harrowing of hell." Satan thought that the crucifixion of Jesus was his greatest victory over God and His redemptive plan. At the moment of Jesus' death and the descent to the dead, Satan first realizes that the death of Jesus was actually God's plan. In Colossians 2, the Apostle Paul describes this when he declares that at the death of Jesus, He *"disarmed the powers and authorities"* and *"made a public spectacle of them, triumphing over them by the cross"* (2:15). This verse is not a reference to human, political authorities, but to the spiritual forces of evil (Eph. 6:12).

Third, the descent to the dead unites Jesus with the saints from all time in His glorious ascension. Ephesians 4:8 declares, *"When He ascended on high He led captives in His train and gave gifts to men."* This idea of leading "captives" is actually a positive reference to those who have been "captured" by Christ and brought into His victory train or victory celebration. Paul goes on to say, *"What does He ascended mean except that He also descended to the lower earthly regions?"* (Eph. 4:9). When Jesus ascended into Heaven, He did not arrive alone, but with all the redeemed over all time with Him, declaring, *"Here am I, and the children God has given me"* (Heb. 2:13).

It is clear that although this is one of the most neglected aspects of Jesus' ministry, the descent into the place of the dead is crucial to our overall understanding of the way the death and resurrection of Jesus is able to have such far-reaching implications in redeeming the world and defeating Satan and his cosmic forces. We should view Holy Saturday, which falls between Good Friday and Easter Sunday, as a kind of hinge that joins these two great acts of God into a single glorious event of power and redemption.

> *To the dead He then descended, entering to claim His own;*
> *Leading forth a host of captives, casting Satan from his throne.*

CHAPTER SIX

The Third Day He Rose from the Dead

Matthew 28:1–10; Acts 2:22–36, 4:8–10; 1 Cor. 15:3–8

The resurrection of Jesus Christ from the dead is the central proclamation of the Church. We serve a risen savior! Over the years groups have tried to re-focus the Church on something else as the central message of the Church. Some have tried to make the ethic of Jesus or His exemplary life the central proclamation of the Church. Wisely, the Church has rejected this and the heart of our message to the world is still the cross and resurrection of Jesus Christ.

In this devotional I want to highlight three things about the resurrection of Jesus Christ.

First, the Resurrection is the public demonstration of God's victory over sin, death and hell. The Resurrection is God's exclamation point on His triumphant victory, crowning the great redemptive act of the cross and the descent to the dead, or the harrowing of hell. The Resurrection vindicates Jesus' claims that He is the resurrection and the life (John 11:25). The Resurrection vindicates our proclamation that anyone who puts their trust in Him will be saved (John 10:9; Acts 11:14, 15:11, 16:31). To *believe* in Jesus does not simply mean to believe that He lived, or believe that He was a towering ethical teacher or even believe that He was a worker of miracles. Most Muslims, Hindus and Buddhists would believe all those things about Jesus. The distinctive of the Christian faith is that we believe that Jesus is the Risen Lord. We believe that His death and resurrection publicly testifies God's victory over the powers of sin, death and hell. We know that we are forgiven because the power of sin has been broken through the resurrection of Jesus Christ from the dead.

Second, the resurrection of Jesus is the guarantee or "firstfruits" of our future bodily resurrection. Christianity, despite all the popular language to the contrary, does not believe that God is merely "saving souls." God is saving *all* of you—your body, your soul, your mind and your spirit. God redeems the whole person. This radically departs from the Greek or Gnostic idea that downplays the importance of the body and believes that only our souls are being liberated to a higher life. This is why we use the word "*resurrection*," not just "*resuscitation*."

Jesus was not simply resuscitated the way Lazarus was. He was resurrected. This means that He was not simply brought back to life from the dead, but that He was victorious over death and took on a new resurrection body. Lazarus was brought back from the dead, as were at least seven others in the

Bible (Zarephath widow's son [1 Kings 17:17–22], son of Shunammite woman [2 Kings 4:30–37], bones of a dead man [2 Kings 13:21], Lazarus [John 11:38–44], widow of Nain's son [Luke 7:11–17], Jairus' daughter [Matt. 8:28–43], Eutychus [Acts 20:7–12] and Dorcas [Acts 9:36–42]). However, none of these received resurrection bodies. Lazarus, Dorcas, Jairus' daughter and the others eventually died again. Jesus, on the other hand, is the firstfruits of the general resurrection at the end of time. This means that Jesus has actually received His resurrection body, just as we will at the end of time. In Paul's first epistle to the Corinthians, he points out that precisely because Jesus has been resurrected, we have the assurance that we will someday be resurrected as well and, like Jesus, receive our glorified bodies. This is why Paul declares, *"Christ has indeed been raised from the dead, the firstfruits of those who have fallen asleep"* (1 Cor. 15:20). This means that Jesus Christ is the pioneer, or the first, guaranteeing that a full harvest will come at the end of time.

Third, the resurrection of Jesus Christ is what makes Christianity unique among all world religions. Today people commonly say that all religions are basically the same. But, the Apostle Paul teaches that the resurrection of Jesus is the central distinguishing feature of Christianity. In fact, he goes so far as to say that if Jesus has not been raised then all our preaching is totally useless and so is our faith (1 Cor. 15:14). If Christ has not been raised we are liars (1 Cor. 15:15), we are still in our sins (1 Cor. 15:17) and we are to be pitied because we have no hope for the future (1 Cor. 15:19). Paul willingly places the entire credibility of the Christian gospel on the truthfulness of the resurrection of Jesus Christ. Without the Resurrection the Christian gospel is really not that different from Islam, Hinduism or Buddhism. We would be just another human religion struggling to make sense of the transcendence of God, but the difference is that the Christian faith is not merely a human religion. More fundamentally, Christianity is a global proclamation of specific, historic acts that have transpired, demonstrating God's power, grace and love. We are not merely spreading religious ideas that inspire the human race. Christianity is not a pragmatic opiate to help us cope with life better. We are proclaiming historical events upon which the entire history of the world is determined. They do, indeed, have a transformative effect on how we live, but the great proclamation of the gospel is about who God is and what He has done. Buddha is in the grave. Mohammad is in the grave. Confucius is in the grave. Jesus is the Risen Lord. Christ's resurrection is why we sing that great hymn:

Crown Him the Lord of life, who triumphed o'er the grave, and rose victorious in the strife, for those He came to save; His glories now we sing, who died and rose on high; Who died eternal life to bring and lives that death may die!

We serve a living Savior! Because He is the Risen Lord, our preaching is not useless. We have a message to proclaim. That message is not another religious idea, but the Person of the Lord Jesus Christ. We proclaim Him (Col. 1:28)!

On the third day Christ arose, triumphant over death's domain;
Firstfruit of the New Creation, Victor over Satan's reign.

CHAPTER SEVEN

He Ascended into Heaven and Sits at the Right Hand of God the Father Almighty

Matt. 22:44, 26:64; Mark 14:62; Luke 24:50–53; Acts 1:11, 2:33; Heb. 1:3, 10:12–13

Picture the final game of a World Series. Each team has won three games, and this is the final game. It is bottom of the ninth inning. The home team is at the plate, and the score is seven to four against the home team. Although three runs behind, the home team's bases are loaded. At this point, there is no need for any seats in the stadium because everyone is on his or her feet cheering and screaming. The opposing team brings in its best closer. It is the bottom of the ninth, two outs, bases loaded, full count—three balls, two strikes. The visiting team is one pitch from winning the World Series. The crowd is standing up cheering. The name of the batter is Jesus. The pitch comes, then the swing, the crack of the bat, and within one second everyone realizes it is a home run—not just an ordinary home run, but the game-winning grand slam. Can you picture what happens as He rounds the bases and finally comes into home plate? The whole team runs and greets Him as He crosses home plate. Everyone jumps up and down, rejoicing. A mound of bodies pile on top of one another because that grand slam home run won it all: victory is secured, the game is won, the rejoicing can begin.

What does this have to do with the Apostles' Creed? Well, one of the most curious observations about the Christian Church is the neglect of the doctrine of the ascension of Christ. We focus so much on Christ's birth, death and resurrection; why do we neglect His ascension? To return to the baseball analogy—His birth is first base, His death on the cross is second base, His resurrection is third base. Why don't we celebrate the complete trip which brings Him all the way home? At the very point when Satan was so certain of his victory, Jesus hit a grand slam. It was, spiritually speaking, bottom of the ninth with two outs, and the lights had been turned out. Yet, Jesus hit a grand slam and, spiritually speaking, brought us all home with Him. The Apostles' Creed reminds us of the importance of remembering and celebrating the full victory of Christ—and that means the Ascension back to Heaven to sit at the right hand of God the Father Almighty.

Many of you may know a popular chorus that celebrates the full cycle of Jesus coming from Heaven to earth and returning to Heaven again. The verse is:

He came from Heaven to earth to show the way, from the earth to the cross our debt to pay; from the cross to the grave, from the grave to the skies, Lord I lift your name on high!

That chorus by Christian music artist Rick Founds gives the full grand slam! However, as much as I like that chorus, I still think the best Ascension hymn is entitled, *"Hail the Day that Sees Him Rise"* by Charles Wesley.

Hail the day that sees Him rise, to His throne above the skies;
Christ, the Lamb for sinners given, enters now the highest Heaven;
There the glorious triumph waits, lift your heads, eternal gates;
Christ hath conquered death and sin, take the King of glory in.
See! The heavens its Lord receives, yet He loves the earth He leaves;
Though returning to His throne, still He calls the world His own;
See! He lifts His hands above, See! He shows the prints of love;
Hark! His gracious lips bestow, Blessings on His Church below.
Lord, beyond our mortal sight, raise our hearts to reach Thy height,
There Thy face unclouded see, find our Heaven of heavens in Thee.

We serve a risen and ascended Lord! This is what the writer of Hebrews means when it refers to Jesus as having *"passed through the heavens"* (Heb. 4:14). The author references the ascension of Christ. The book of Hebrews tells us three things we need to know about the ascended Lord.

First, He is Waiting (prophet role).

Jesus has been waiting for nearly 2,000 years and counting. His deferment is one of the neglected features of a prophet in the Old Testament. Once the prophets delivered their word, they waited to see if the people repented or hardened their hearts. We don't often think about God waiting, but this is the language of Scripture itself. Jesus waits for the full consummation of His victory to be realized. The victory has been secured, but not everyone sees it, knows it and believes it. We have all heard stories about Japanese soldiers who were still fighting WWII years after Japan surrendered. The world is in a similar situation. Jesus is the Risen Lord who sits at the right hand of God the Father Almighty. But not everyone knows about or acknowledges His victory. Many remain in conflict with the Lordship of Jesus Christ.

Hebrews 10:12b-13 says, *"He sat down at the right hand of God. Since that time He waits for His enemies to be made His footstool."* Jesus waits for the full consummation, realization or culmination of His work to be fully known. The Scripture says that someday *"every knee shall bow and every tongue confess that Jesus Christ is Lord to the Glory of God the Father"* (Phil. 2:10–11).

Second, He is Interceding (priestly role).

Jesus fulfills the Jewish priesthood. The priests were the ones set apart by God to enter the holy of holies to intercede on behalf of the people by praying and offering the blood of the sacrifice on the mercy seat of the ark of the covenant. No ordinary person, even an ordinary Jewish person, could presume to be a priest. According to the Law, only members of the tribe of Levi could be priests. But even those priests only fulfilled certain functions, (sacrificing animals, caring for the temple, distributing money to help the poor etc . . .). Only a certain class of Levites who were also the direct descendents of Aaron, the brother of Moses, could become High Priests. Only the High Priest could enter the holy of holies, and he could only do it once per year on the Day of Atonement.

Hebrews declares seven reasons why Jesus' priesthood is superior to the Jewish priesthood. Read each of these carefully and take a moment to reflect on each of them. These thoughts will deepen your appreciation for the greatness of the priesthood of Jesus Christ.

(1) Their priesthood was based on human ancestry, whereas Jesus' priesthood is based on the power of His indestructible life (Heb. 7:16).

(2) Their priesthood was temporary whereas Jesus' priesthood is permanent (Heb. 7:27, 10:6).

(3) Their priesthood only entered into an earthly, holy place, whereas Jesus' priesthood enters into the heavens into the very presence of the Father (Heb. 8:1–2).

(4) Their priesthood had to sacrifice for their own sins and then the sins of the people, whereas Jesus' priesthood is undefiled because He is without sin (Heb. 7:23–25).

(5) Their priesthood offered sacrifices that had to be repeated over and over again, whereas Jesus' priesthood offers the sacrifice of Himself once and for all (Heb. 10:1–4).

(6) Their priest offered sacrifices that actually had no power to take away sin, whereas Jesus offered Himself as the perfect undefiled sacrifice (Heb. 10:11).

(7) They were Jewish Priests in the order of Aaron and could only intercede for fellow Jews, whereas Jesus is a priest for all peoples and for all nations in the order of Melchizedek (Heb.5:6, 7:17).

A prophet is one who faces the people and proclaims God's Word to them. A priest, in contrast, faces God and intercedes on behalf of the people. Jesus is both the perfect prophet and the perfect priest. As the perfect priest, Jesus is the perfect intercessor. Scripture declares that Jesus fulfills this role, saying, *"Now there were many of those priests, since death prevented them from continuing in office; but because Jesus lives forever, He has a permanent priesthood. Therefore, He is able to save completely those who come to God through Him, because He always lives to intercede for them"* (Heb. 7:23–25). It is truly amazing to think that Jesus lived on this earth for thirty-three years, but He has been interceding for His Church for more than 2,000 years.

Third, He is Reigning (kingly role).

The Scripture says that when Jesus ascended He *"sat down at the right hand of God"* (Mark 16:19; Heb. 1:3, 10:12, 12:2; Matt. 26:64; Mark 14:62; Luke 22:69; Acts 2:33, 5:31, 7:55f; Romans 8:34; 1 Peter 3:22; Rev. 5:1, 7). Jesus' position with God is a very dominant theme in Scripture, and that precise language was carried over into the Creed. This role of Jesus sitting at the right hand of God the Father where He makes intercession for us is known as the *session of the Son.* What does it mean for Jesus to be seated on a throne at the right hand of the Father? This language conveys that Jesus rules and reigns over all. He is sovereign in power, glory and majesty. His sovereignty is why the Apostle Paul says that *"every knee should bow"* and *"every tongue confess that Jesus Christ is Lord to the glory of God the Father"* (Phil. 2:10–11). Christ rules and reigns, which is why the very earliest confession of faith in the Church was the three-word phrase, *"Jesus is Lord"* (1 Cor. 12:3).

Now when we think of Jesus ruling and reigning at the "right hand of God," we should not think of this in spatial terms, as if Jesus is sitting on a great big chair in a large throne room in Heaven. Or at least we should not think of it *only* in those terms. The "right hand of God" is a much bigger concept than simply a physical location. These words are a way of expressing that Jesus is actively present and extends the rule and reign of God in *every* place in the whole universe. So when Jesus rose from the dead and ascended, He reassumed the full exercise of His prerogatives as the second person of the Trinity. When Jesus became incarnate, He accepted the spatial limitations of a human body. If Jesus were in Galilee, He physically could not be in Nazareth. Today, Jesus is omnipresent in His Church and, indeed, wherever *"two or more are gathered"* in His name (Matt. 18:20). Thus, when Jesus ascended into Heaven, He ascended from here to everywhere, not simply from here to another location. This is why the presence of Jesus can be with us when we pray, as well as commune with us as we receive the Lord's Supper and so forth.

In conclusion, the ascension of Christ brings the full power of Jesus' incarnation, death and resurrection "home," revealing how Jesus fulfills the role of prophet, priest and king. It's a grand slam!

Christ ascended into Heaven, seated at the Father's hand;
For our lives He's interceding till on earth He takes His stand.

CHAPTER EIGHT

From There, He Shall Come to Judge the Living and the Dead.

John 5:22; 2 Tim. 4:1; 1 Cor. 3:11–15; 1 Thes. 4:13–18; 2 Thes. 1:5–10

Introduction

Bob Mumford, a popular Bible teacher, once shared how he had experienced a very disturbing dream. In the dream he saw his Bible lying on the top of his desk in his study. He sat down and he opened his Bible, only to find that in the dream his Bible has somehow changed. It was a very unusual Bible. Even though all the same books of the Bible were there, some of the pages of the Bible were huge pages, far bigger than you would expect. Yet, as he turned the pages of his Bible in the dream he came across other pages in his Bible that were very tiny. As he flipped through the pages of his Bible, the whole Bible was this way, some pages supersized and other pages so miniscule he could hardly see the page to turn. Then in the dream, he sensed the Lord speaking to him, saying, "Bob preach my whole Word, not just your favorite parts!" Then, Bob awoke from the dream. I wonder what our Bibles would look like if they were miraculously changed to reflect which verses we read and quote and which verses we overlook?

Humans have a natural tendency to avoid the difficult and challenging parts of Scripture and only read the uplifting, encouraging passages. Today's emphasis on "seeker sensitive" churches has sometimes reinforced this problem. Some churches plan "home on the range" services. This refers to services where everything is happy and "seldom is heard a discouraging word." But the Apostles' Creed calls us to remember the entire gospel, not just our favorite parts. This next phrase in the Apostles' Creed reminds us that Jesus *"shall come to judge the living and the dead."* I hope this devotional helps us to see that not only is this a theme that we should not ignore, but it is also one of the most precious doctrines of the Church. Indeed, God's judgment against the wicked and His sovereign decree to set all things right that have been skewed by sin and evil is a great source of hope for Christians. Far from our not wanting to discuss God's righteous judgment, we should long for it, wait expectantly for it and find in it a source of comfort and peace.

Return of Christ

The first part of the phrase "He shall come" refers to the fact that at some point Jesus Christ will manifest Himself and all earthly, human history as we know it will come to an end. This end will be inaugurated through the glorious return of Jesus Christ. Jesus Himself said that *"at that time the Son of Man will appear in the sky, and all the nations of the earth will mourn. They will see the Son of Man coming on the clouds of the sky, with great power and great glory."* (Matt. 24:30). He goes on to say that there will be a great trumpet call, and He will send His angels to gather His Church from the ends of the earth (Matt. 2:31). The Apostle Paul teaches the same truth in 1 Thessalonians 4:15-16 when he says, *"For the Lord Himself will come down from Heaven, with a loud command, with the voice of the archangel and with the trumpet call of God, and the dead in Christ will rise first."* His return will be personal and physical. Paul calls the return of Christ the *"blessed hope"* of the Church (Titus 2:13).

Single, unified return

Some Christians teach that Christ's return will be in two stages—a secret coming "for His saints" and, after some years of tribulation, a public return "with His saints." This idea has been popularized recently by the *Left Behind Series*. Despite the popularity of these books, it is important to point out that the likelihood that a doctrine of a secret rapture is actually taught in Scripture is remote. Indeed, dozens and dozens of biblical references make it very difficult to sustain this doctrine, even though it is very popular and widely believed. It is true that at the moment of Christ's glorious return we will be caught up—or raptured—to meet Him in the clouds. This celestial meeting pictures what we all do when someone important comes to visit, arriving at a nearby airport. We go out "to meet" them and then return with the guest to our home. We go up "to meet" the Lord as He descends, but not so we can be whisked away to some other place, but so we can return with Christ to a renewed earth. In other words, Christ's return is one, great, climatic and public event. The imagery of the thief coming in the night is not to emphasize its *secrecy*, but rather its *surprise*. The world is not expecting Christ's return any more than someone expects a thief to come in the night. The point is the *unexpectedness* of it. However, when it occurs, every eye will see Him. His arrival will not go unnoticed. In fact, the Greek word used to describe Christ's coming is the word *"parousia"* which means "glorious appearance."

Judgment Day

Jesus returns to vindicate His saints and to judge the world. For this reason, the Apostles' Creed says, "He will come to judge the living and the dead." Judgment Day is coming for us all. In Romans 14:10 Paul says, *"For we will all stand before the Judgment Seat of God."* Several events will take place on Judgment Day, though the order or sequence of these events, as well as the timing, is not completely clear. However, three aspects of the final judgment are clear.

First, Judgment Day will reveal and make known all sins. The secrets of everyone's heart will be revealed. Romans 2:16 says, *"This will take place on the day when God will judge men's secrets."* Every thought, every idle word, every deed—even deeds done in absolute secrecy—will be made known and laid bare. Jesus says in Luke 12:2-3, *"There is nothing concealed that will not be disclosed, or* *hidden that will not be made known. What you have said in the dark will be heard in the daylight, and what you have whispered in the ear in the inner rooms will be proclaimed from the housetops.*" Crimes which people thought they had "gotten away with" will suddenly be known. All sins will be revealed and publicly exposed. Judgment is actually good news because it means that everything will be "set right." Judgment is about God setting things right. Today people commonly express that they believe in a "God of love;" therefore, they cannot accept the idea that God "would ever judge anyone." However, crucial to the biblical doctrine of God's love is that all things will eventually be set right. Love without justice is mere sentimentality.

Judgment at the end of time must be seen and understood in the larger context that God has taken upon Himself, through Christ, the righteous judgment which sinners deserved. Jesus bore our sins on the cross. He accepted the full weight of the guilty verdict. Now, through the gospel, the entire world is invited to receive that gift of grace.

Second, Judgment Day will vindicate the faith of the Church. Praise God that the record of sins is not the only book in Heaven. There is another book that holds a record of all those who have placed their faith in Jesus Christ. For the believer, Judgment Day becomes transformed from a day of fear and trial, to a day of vindication and joy. The Scripture says that the name of that other book is known as the *Lamb's Book of Life*. That book will reveal the names of those people whose sins have already been paid because of their trust in the provision offered through the gospel of our Lord Jesus

Christ. The Church will be vindicated, not because we are without sin, but because of our perseverance in faith. This truth is celebrated in the song that says, "He paid a debt He did not owe, I owed a debt I could not pay, Christ Jesus came and washed my sins away!"

Third, righteous rewards will be granted to the people of God. God will honor those who have served Christ faithfully. We are not told the precise nature of these rewards, but the Apostle Paul writes in 1 Corinthians 3 that everything we have ever done or said as Christians will be subjected to some kind of holy fire. This fire will test, as in a furnace, the true quality of our labors. This evaluation is not a test of the unbelievers, for all of their works fall to the ground because the Bible says that whatever is not done from faith is sin. Therefore, the unbelieving dead have no reward, but can only expect eternal judgment. However, not all believers have lived before God with the same degree of faithfulness, and this, too, will become known.

Paul begins by establishing that this is only in reference to the believer when he says, *"For no one can lay any foundation other than the one already laid, which is Jesus Christ."* Then he goes on to talk about what we do in our Christian lives. *"If any person builds on this foundation using gold, sliver, costly stones, wood, hay or straw, their work will be shown for what it is, because the Day* (Judgment Day) *will bring it to light. It will be revealed with fire, and the fire will test the quality of each person's work. If what he has built survives, he will receive his reward. If it is burned up, he will suffer loss; he himself will be saved, but only as one escaping through the flames"* (1 Cor. 3:11–15). This is not a test for salvation. We cannot save ourselves through good works. Only Christ can save us. However, we have been saved for good works. Paul says, *"By grace you been saved, through faith . . . it is the gift of God . . . for we are God's workmanship, created in Christ Jesus to do good works* (Eph. 2:8–10).

So, let us rejoice this day in the great provision which God has made in Jesus Christ. But, let us also remember that the good news of the gospel is not just that we are saved, but also that we can rest in peace knowing that despite all of the evil and wickedness in the world, God will someday set everything right.

> *Jesus Christ will come again to judge the living and the dead;*
> *Then the world will be made right when under Him, our living head.*

CHAPTER NINE

I Believe in the Holy Spirit

John 15:26, 16:7–14; Acts 2:1–4, 13:2

The next phrase of the Apostles' Creed, *"I believe in the Holy Spirit,"* decisively places the Trinity at the heart of Christian proclamation. The Creed began, "I believe in God, the Father *Almighty*," and then asserted, "And in *Jesus Christ*, His only Son, our Lord." Now, the Creed affirms, "I believe in the *Holy Spirit*." This is the crowning glory of the Christian proclamation. The Trinity is not some kind of speculative doctrine that only theologians discuss. The Trinity lies at the heart of our faith and worship. Without the Trinity all of the core doctrines of Christianity become incoherent.

In order to appreciate the role of the Holy Spirit and the Trinity, we must see how it finally reconciles two twin truths about God. On the one hand, God is high and holy. He dwells in unapproachable light. On the other hand, this very God of majestic, unspeakable power and holiness has also revealed Himself to us in tenderness and compassion. The same God who revealed

His holiness also declares, "*Can a mother forget the baby at her breast and have no compassion on the child she has borne? Though she may forget, I will not forget you! See, I have engraved you on the palms of my hands . . .*" (Isa. 49:15–16). God Himself sums up these twin truths when He speaks through the prophet Isaiah and declares, "*I dwell in a high and holy place, and also with him who is humble and lowly in spirit*" (Isa. 57:15). God dwells in two places: in the high and holy place, and also in the place of humbleness and humility.

The Trinity as the Highest Conception of God

Only the doctrine of the Trinity has the capacity to embrace the full range of these great twin mysteries. Through the Trinity, the Father reigns in majesty from His throne, even while His Son, in lowliness, suffers and dies upon the cross. I am convinced that a church that does not preach the Triune God, even if they speak of Jesus regularly, will eventually lose a proper view of God's true holiness. Indeed, to most people today, a sense of awe comes only with the greatest difficulty. For many Christians, God has become domesticated and put in a box so that we can pull Him out when we need Him. As Philip Yancey observed, we have domesticated angels into stuffed toys and Christmas ornaments. We have made jokes about Peter at the pearly gates, and even Easter has been tamed into plastic green grass and bunny rabbits. The awe of the shepherds and the reverence of the wise men have been traded for a jolly Santa Claus, tiny reindeer and elves. Even Almighty God is referred to as "The Man Upstairs." Worship has become synonymous with music. We need to catch a renewed glimpse of the glory and majesty of the Triune God.

The Trinity is also important because it reveals that God's very nature is relational. God has eternal relationships within Himself. The Puritans used to say that "God in Himself is a sweet society." Islam teaches that God is solitary and has no interest in revealing Himself to us. Hinduism believes that the highest conception of God is abstract and impersonal. Buddhism does not believe in an ultimate God, only lesser enlightened beings. The Trinity is unique to the Christian proclamation. Trinity is just a shorthand version of Tri-unity, i.e. three in one. The Church believes that God has revealed Himself in three eternal distinctions, Father, Son and Holy Spirit, but that these three are One. One God in three persons, blessed Trinity.

What does it mean for the Church to confess faith in the Holy Spirit?

First, the Holy Spirit endues the Church with God's authority. The Holy Spirit is not merely an impersonal force. Rather, the Holy Spirit is the authoritative, empowering presence of the living God. The gospel doesn't *stop* at the cross, resurrection and ascension of Christ. The gospel continues to unfold in the coming of the Spirit at Pentecost. The Holy Spirit is the ongoing reminder that God does not just exercise authority *over* the world, but He has authority to act *in* the world.

The Spirit empowers us and sanctifies us for effective service and witness (Acts 2). The Spirit intercedes with us and within us, teaching us effective prayer (Rom. 8). The Holy Spirit teaches, instructs and admonishes us as we read the Scriptures (John 16:13). The Spirit applies and nurtures the fruits of the Spirit (which is the character of Christ) in our lives—love, joy, peace, patience, kindness, goodness, gentleness, faithfulness and self-control. The Spirit gives us direction and guidance in life (Acts 13:2, 16:6 and Rom. 8:14). Indeed, our lives, our vocations, our every breath becomes a radiant reflection of God's work in and through His Spirit.

Even before we become Christians, the Spirit convicts the world regarding sin. You would have no consciousness of sin apart from the ministry of the Holy Spirit. The Holy Spirit is the one who knocks at the door of our hearts and bathes us in God's prevenient grace, reminding us that we need a savior. If you are a Christian, you had no power to open the door of your heart to Jesus Christ without the prompting and enablement of the Holy Spirit. Paul says, *"You were dead in your trespasses and sins."* (Eph. 2:1). Sin is not merely a ball and chain that impedes our progress. We are dead and have no power to save ourselves unless the Holy Spirit intervenes with God's prevenient grace in our lives, enabling us to hear the gospel and put our faith in Jesus Christ.

Second, the Holy Spirit empowers the Church for global mission. Just prior to His ascension, Jesus tells His disciples to wait until they have been *"baptized with the Holy Spirit"* (Acts 1:5). Jesus goes on to say that we will receive power and we will be His witnesses to the ends of the earth (Acts 1:8). Through the Holy Spirit the people of the Church are empowered to be effective witnesses unto Christ. We have a responsibility to bring the gospel to every remaining people-group in the entire world. Studies estimate that there are approximately 24,000 distinct ethnic groups in the world. Thousands of those groups do not yet have a credible witness of the gospel. Almost one billion people in the world have never heard the good news of Jesus Christ.

Third, the Holy Spirit extends the in-breaking of the New Creation through powerful manifestations of signs and wonders and holiness of life. The ministry of the Church is to reflect the ministry of Jesus. The Spirit delivers the *not yet* into the *already*. That means that the future realities that we normally associate only with Heaven (healing, reconciliation, deliverance, etc.) are already breaking into the world through the Spirit. Men and women are healed by the power of God. They experience reconciliation with one another. The poor and downtrodden receive hope. Sin is brought under conviction. Redemption is wrought.

Is it any wonder that the Apostle Paul exhorts us in Ephesians 5:18, *"Don't get drunk with wine, but be filled with the Holy Spirit!"*

When you become a Christian, the first two things you should do is get baptized in water and then pray to receive the full indwelling of the Holy Spirit.

> *I believe the Triune God is Father, Holy Spirit, Son;*
> *I believe the Holy Spirit is with them forever one.*

CHAPTER TEN

The Holy Catholic Church,
the Communion of Saints

**Matt. 16:18; Acts 13:1–3, 14:21–23; 1 Cor. 12:27–31;
Gal. 3:26–29; Heb. 10:25**

The Apostles' Creed makes the Church an article of faith: We believe in the holy catholic Church. This statement means that we *believe* in the Church in the same way we *believe* in the death of Christ or His resurrection. This belief is important because it lifts the Church from being a mere human organization that has certain functions, such as preaching, discipling or feeding the hungry. Instead, the Church is what God is building in the world. The Church is God's divine work built on the foundation of Christ. Jesus said, "*I will build my Church*" (Matt. 16:18). The Church does not exist because it is the most efficient organization that we have come up with, and if we can think of a more efficient way to do the tasks that the Church does, then we can abandon the Church and start a different kind of organization. No! The

Church *is* what God is doing in the world. The Church is a divine work, the bride of Christ, the gathered community of the redeemed.

The Church is the divinely established community, which alone is to exhibit all the realities of the coming age into the present. In other words, all the future realities of the New Creation, such as reconciliation, worship, healing, joy and so forth, are to be already present in the community God has established, namely the Church. The Church does not merely do these things; the Church *is* the thing God is building to manifest His presence and glory in the world.

This phrase of the Apostles' Creed points out two qualities of the Church: namely, that it is *holy* and that it is *catholic*. To be *holy* means to be set apart. The Church has been set apart for righteousness, godliness and beauty, i.e. a spotless bride for Christ. Holiness is one of the central messages of the Methodist-Wesleyan movement around the world. Luther and the early Reformers of the sixteenth century taught the doctrine of *alien righteousness*. This doctrine means that we are saved through the righteousness of Christ alone and that through faith God graciously imputes or graciously gives to us the righteousness of Christ. We are therefore *righteous* or *holy* but only because Christ is righteous and holy. The emphasis on holiness, however, reminds us that *alien righteousness* is not God's last word for the Church. It is true that we are justified by God imputing Christ's righteousness to us. It is foreign and alien to us. However, salvation is about more than justification. Righteousness for Wesley was about more than God just looking at us through a different set of glasses. Alien righteousness must become native righteousness. Imputed righteousness must become actualized righteousness. Declared righteousness must become embodied righteousness, wrought in us not by our own strength but through the power of the living God. The Church is not merely to be "declared holy;" we are to *be* holy.

The second word used to describe the Church is the word *catholic*. This word has been misunderstood because people often confuse this word as a reference to the Roman Catholic Church. However, the word *catholic* in this context means *universal*. The Creed should display the word catholic with a lower case *c*, not an upper case C, which would imply the Roman Catholic Church. It is our confession that the Church of Jesus Christ has burst forth from the parochial, swaddling clothes of our Jewish origin and is now a global movement of all tongues, tribes and nations. In this section of the Creed, we remember that we are first and foremost not Methodists, Baptists, Presbyterians or Pentecostals. We are first Christians. We belong to the worldwide body of Christ that stretches back through time and space around the world. This is why we call the Apostles' Creed an ecumenical creed and not a statement of faith. The Creed says nothing about the particularities of being a Baptist or a Methodist or a Roman Catholic Christian. This does not mean that these distinctions are not important—even vitally important. However, what it does mean is that these distinctions are secondary to our first identity as Christians.

The phrase "the communion of the saints" is, like the word *catholic*, another indicator of our identity with all Christians everywhere and back through time. Whereas the word *catholic* emphasizes our global identity with all Christians all over the world, the "communion of the saints" emphasizes our spiritual connection with the Church throughout space and time. To be "in communion" with someone means to be spiritually connected with a shared fellowship under the Lordship of Jesus Christ. In the New Testament to share communion or fellowship with someone means three things.

First, shared fellowship means that we share a common confession. We all affirm the Apostolic proclamation of the Lordship of Jesus Christ. The Apostle John asks, *"Who is the liar but he who denies that Jesus is the Christ? This is the antichrist, he who denies the Father and the Son. No one who denies the Son has the Father. Whoever confesses the Son has the Father also."* (1 John 2:22–23). When modern day liberal groups stop confessing and proclaiming the Lordship and supremacy of Jesus Christ they are, in effect, breaking fellowship or communion with the saints through time.

Second, to be in communion with the saints refers to a mystical connection we have with one another and with Christ since we are called the "body of Christ" (Col. 1:18). Paul expresses this when he says that *"we, though many, are one body in Christ, and individually members one of another"* (Rom. 12:5). The idea of being mystically connected as a "body" to Christ's headship or to be "members one of another" expresses a deep level of communion that we do not often appreciate as Christians. We are not merely individual believers who have been baptized and confessed our faith in Christ and have a "personal relationship with Christ." This language is not wrong.

Rather, this language is too weak, too tepid to express the fullness of the biblical vision of what it means to be called and adopted into His family.

Third, the phrase "communion of the saints" reminds us that the Church is, in its essence, not an institution or some bureaucratic structure with a complex organizational chart. The Church is a community of redeemed *people*. Despite popular language to the contrary, we cannot *go* to church. This language is foreign to Scripture. Rather, we assemble *as* the Church (1 Cor. 11:18). When we are baptized, we do not merely confess our personal faith in Christ as we are baptized "into Christ." We are also baptized *into His body* (Rom. 6:3–4). We become connected to one another. This is also expressed in the Lord's Supper that is, quite rightly, often known as *communion*. This means that when we partake of the Lord's Supper we are not only reinforcing our communion or connection with Christ, but also our connection with one another. This is why we do not come to the Lord's Supper if we are not living in forgiveness and reconciliation with our brothers and sisters in Christ.

This portion of the Apostles' Creed celebrates our *togetherness* as Christians under the Lordship of Jesus Christ. We fight hard against the headwinds of denominational sectarianism, individualism and disunity. The Creed is God's gracious way of reminding us of that which unites us.

I believe there is one holy Church for whom Christ bled and died;
Saints throughout the world and time who have communion as His bride.

CHAPTER ELEVEN

The Forgiveness of Sins

Matt. 26:28; Luke 7:48, 24:47;
Acts 2:38, 5:31, 10:43, 13:38, 26:18; Col. 1:14; Heb. 9:22

Up to this point, the Apostles' Creed has declared who God is and what He has done. For example, we affirm that God the Father Almighty created the heavens and the earth and that Jesus Christ suffered under Pontius Pilate and so forth. This might be called news, even divinely disclosed news. However, at *this* point in the Creed we see that this is good news *for us*. We now learn the implications of all of God's actions for us: forgiveness of sins and life everlasting. This chapter focuses on the phrase, "forgiveness of sins."

The Old Testament had a provision for the forgiveness of sins, but it was partial and incomplete. When the Old Testament believers sacrificed a bull or a goat in God's presence it was like signing a promissory note with a bank. The document is signed today, promising full payment at some point in the future. The definition of a promissory note is "a written promise to pay at a fixed future time a sum of money to a specified individual." You receive the benefits immediately, but you have promised a future payment. If you do not pay off the debt at the fixed future point, then you are in default and what you have received will be taken away from you and penalties or imprisonment will be incurred.

This is exactly what God did in the Old Testament. He essentially said that there are millions of people who are going to live before the coming of my Son, Jesus Christ. A provision must be made for them; but it will be like a promissory note. Forgiveness will be granted now, but it will be tied to a future payment. The Lord says, in effect, I will temporarily accept the blood of bulls and goats offered by faith in the Temple through the priesthood. However, the blood of bulls and goats anticipates and, indeed, requires a future payment. Hebrews 10:4 is quite explicit: *"It is impossible for the blood of bulls and goats to take away sins."* Impossible—even though the Scriptures commanded it. Hebrews 10:11 says, *"Day after day every priest stands and performs his religious duties; again and again he offers the same sacrifices, which can never take away sins."* Why? Because the blood of bulls and goats was not actually a payment for sins; it was a promise of a future payment. The animal blood served as a pledge to God in the present—offered in faith—that a future provision would actually satisfy the debt.

So even though the Old Testament believers experienced forgiveness, their sins were not taken away or washed away. They were temporarily covered up and overlooked in anticipation of a future payment. That final payment came through Jesus Christ. So, from this perspective we realize that the Old Testament believers were not saved through some alternative means as is often assumed to be the case. Abraham, Noah, Daniel and Hezekiah and all the rest of the Old Testament saints were saved precisely the same way we are: namely, *through Jesus Christ and His death on the cross.* The only difference is that they had promissory notes and had to die in anticipation of a future payment, whereas we can look back on a payment that has already been rendered. In that sense it is different, but the provision of Jesus Christ worked simultaneously back through time as well as forward through time. (This is one of the reasons Jesus descended into Hades as we discussed in chapter five. He announced that all sacrifices made in faith had now been paid in full). If Christ had not died upon the cross, every sacrifice in the Old Testament would have gone into default and every prayer of faith which we have prayed would be in default. The result would have been the equivalent of a massive, global spiritual bankruptcy because no one could be found to pay the debt.

This is why even devout Jewish believers who were the first followers of Christ saw that the Law was only *"a shadow of the good things that are coming—not the realities themselves"* (Heb. 10:1). The writer of Hebrews goes on to demonstrate why forgiveness in the Old Testament is dependent upon Christ's later work on the cross and cannot stand on its own feet apart from Christ.

First, the sacrifices had to be endlessly repeated, whereas Christ offered up Himself once for all. The Scripture says, *"But when this priest had* *offered for all time one sacrifice for sins, He sat down at the right hand of God (the Father)"* (Heb. 10:12), because *"by one sacrifice He has made perfect forever those who are being made holy"* (10:14).

Second, the sacrifices merely covered sin up, they did not actually take it away. In the Old Testament the word *"atonement"* means "to cover," whereas in the New Testament the word *"forgiveness"* means "to take away or to remove."

Third, the Old Testament focused on forgiving outward acts of disobedience, whereas the New Testament focuses on cleansing the heart of all guilt and shame. The Old Testament focused on pardoning rebellious acts. The New Testament focuses on restoring a broken relationship. The Old Testament is symbolized by the tablets of stone and the heavy veil which separated the holy of holies from the worshipper. These are external things. The New Testament focuses on the transformation of the human heart and restoring the believer into intimate communion with God and His Church. The New Testament is the fulfillment of the promise, *"This is the covenant I will make with them . . . I will put my law within them, and I will write it on their hearts"* (Jer. 31:33). This verse is a reference to the power of forgiveness that cleanses us within, makes us holy and fills us with the Holy Spirit, God's divine presence in the life of the believer.

How do we respond to this incredible good news made possible through Jesus' death on the cross? Jesus first declares this good news and then tells us how to respond. We as the forgiven, reconciled people of God respond by forgiving those who have sinned against us. Remember, He is determined that we be like Him. We who have been forgiven become like Him by becoming forgivers. In fact, if we will not forgive those who have sinned against us, then we have not actually heard the good news of our own forgiveness. God is not just reconciling individual sinners to Himself, He is reconciling us to one another and, indeed, ultimately with the whole of creation.

Jesus tells the parable in Matthew 18 of the man who owed a king what, in our currency, amounts to millions of dollars. He was thrown into prison, along with his wife and children, but he fell on his knees and begged for mercy. The king had compassion on him and cancelled the entire debt. The king declared that his debt was completely forgiven, and he was let out of debtors' prison. But as he left prison and was walking down the street, he met a man who owed him the equivalent of three dollars. He had only a few minutes earlier been forgiven millions, but he responded to that good news by choking the man who owed him three dollars and demanding full payment. When the king heard this, he was so outraged he had the man re-arrested and thrown back into prison where he belonged because he had, quite obviously, not really received the extraordinary gift in the first place.

We demonstrate that we have received forgiveness by becoming forgivers ourselves. This is why Ephesians 4:32 says, *"Forgive each other just as in Christ God forgave you."* This is why Colossians 3:13 says, *"Bear with each other and forgive whatever grievances you may have against one another. Forgive as the Lord forgave you.*" This is why our Lord teaches us in the Lord's prayer, *"Forgive us our trespasses as we forgive those who trespass against us"* (Matt. 6:12). You see, the two are linked. This is why Jesus goes on in that passage to say, *"For if you forgive men when they sin against you, your heavenly father will forgive you. But if you do not forgive men their sins, your father will not forgive your sins"* (Matt. 6:14–15). Scripture makes it absolutely clear that our capacity to receive God's forgiveness is linked to our forgiving others.

Is there someone in your life you need to call or write and ask for forgiveness this day? This may involve making restitution. Is there someone whom you yourself need to forgive? It may be someone who has already died. If that is the case, you must still do it before God, declaring them forgiven. Sometimes the person we have to forgive is ourselves. Many people are able to freely accept God's grace in the lives of others, but will not receive it for themselves. Hear the good news—in the name of Jesus Christ, you are forgiven! Let go of those chains that bind you in bitterness, fear and unforgiveness. Only then can the good news really be the good news for you. The provision has been made, but like any gift, you must receive it and open it. The only way to open the gift of forgiveness is to give it away yourself.

Wondrous gift of sins' forgiveness, purchased at a costly price;
Freely must be giv'n to others, honoring Christ's sacrifice.

CHAPTER TWELVE

The Resurrection of the Body and the Life Everlasting

John 6:39, 10:28, 11:25, 17:2–3; Acts 24:10–15; 1 Cor. 15:12–58; 1 Thes. 4:16

I believe in the Resurrection of the body and the life everlasting! What a triumphant way for the Apostles' Creed to end. After all, the Apostles' Creed is no mere dry, dusty statement of doctrines. It is the Church's historic summary of our proclamation to the world about the good news of the gospel of our Lord Jesus Christ! The Creed reminds the Church of our destiny. Our bodies, which lie in the grave, will be resurrected at the end of time; they will be gloriously transformed, and we will dwell with the Triune God forever.

Christians believe in a bodily resurrection. As discussed in chapter six, we do not believe simply in a spiritual state where our souls live forever. In contrast, Christianity affirms that our entire life, which includes our bodies, our minds, our souls and our spirits, is to be redeemed. In fact, the Apostle

Paul is so determined to establish the Christian view of the resurrection body that he links the resurrection of our bodies in the future with the resurrection of Jesus Christ in the past. Paul teaches that if Christ has not been raised, then we also will not be raised. If Christ has not been raised, then we have no hope. We are to be pitied; we are still in our sins. In 1 Corinthians 15:16 Paul says, *"For if the dead are not raised, then Christ has not been raised either."* The whole certainty of our faith in the general, bodily resurrection at the end of time is linked to the bodily resurrection of Jesus Christ. This is why the Apostles' Creed first declares, "On the third day He rose again from the dead!" The resurrection of Christ is the key and the foundation for our resurrection from the dead. In 1 Corinthians 15:20 Paul declares, *"But Christ has indeed been raised from the dead, the first fruits of those who have fallen asleep."* Notice how he avoids the word *"death"* because *death* has a finality to it—and in Christ, death does not have the final word. The Bible refers to the first death and the second death. The first death is the one we know about. This death refers to the fact that our bodies are decaying and rushing toward the grave. One day you wake up and notice that you don't run up steps like you used to. You might notice some aches and pains that weren't there before. These are gentle reminders that our bodies in their present form are not built for eternity. We may dye our hair, watch our weight or exercise vigorously, but we all know that our bodies in their present form are dying. Unless Christ returns in our lifetime, we will someday all die. This is the first death. But the Scriptures speak of a second death in Revelation 20:6. This refers to eternal death apart from Christ. For the believer in Christ, the second death has no power over us. Our sins have already been judged in Christ. They have been paid for through the power of the cross and we are not subject to eternal judgment. So, once that is removed Paul doesn't even want to use the word *death* for us—he simply evokes a euphemism and says, "those who have fallen asleep." For us, our physical death is like falling asleep. In other words, it is like sleep in the sense that one day we will wake up to a new Day, but not just any day—the Day of Resurrection.

Christians believe that our resurrected body will be a splendorous, glorious body. While continuities exist between our present body and the resurrected body, our new body is mostly a transformed body (1 Cor. 15:35–42). Paul likens it to a kernel of corn compared with the full stalk. As we discussed in chapter six, this is a resurrection, not resuscitation.

Resurrection is far more than just a re-tooling of the body we have. This will not be like one of those famous "before" and "after" shots on a diet commercial. This is a splendorous transformation that we can hardly imagine.

> *The body that is sown is perishable, it is raised imperishable;*
> *It is sown in dishonor (sickness and weakness), it is raised in glory;*
> *It is sown in weakness, it is raised in power;*
> *It is sown a natural body, it is raised a spiritual body.*

Your resurrection body will be imperishable, not subject to decay. It will be glorious. It will be powerful. It is called a spiritual body, which brings together two words into one phrase—body and spirit. It is an unusual combination, but it is not a mere spiritual existence; it is a bodily existence which is constantly vivified and empowered through His spiritual life. We will live forever because our life is tied to His life, and since God cannot die, we will not die—but will enjoy an everlasting life.

The last phrase of the Creed expresses our faith in "life everlasting." That phrase should not be heard as a kind of never-ending static existence. The fact that we will no longer be subject to sickness or decay does not mean that we will be static. To have everlasting life does not mean merely that we never get sick again and, therefore, our new bodies won't wear out. Rather, we should see our eternality rooted in that fact that we have been joined and united with Christ for all eternity. It is our union with Christ that is the source of our everlasting life, not just that we have been given really good new bodies.

Also, the word *"life"* here does not mean merely that we continue to *exist*. Rather, *life* means that we experience the fullness of the original purpose of our creation. In the New Creation we will be engaged in all the kinds of industrious work, projects, inventions and building that we are involved with here, *but without the presence of sin*. Indeed, this is the great transforming fact about the New Creation. It is not a spirit-type existence where we sit endlessly on a cloud with the wings of an angel, or stand forever in a worship service that never has a benediction. Rather, we should see that all of life becomes an act of worship, and the absence of sin completely transforms the very nature of life and work. We will be unleashed into endless creativity and deeper discoveries about God's creation. For all eternity we will be brought deeper and deeper into the full glory and mystery of the Trinity and His self-revelation. We will learn to love Him and one another in deeper and deeper ways. We will, ultimately, be like Him because we will finally see Him face to face. As John says, *"Beloved, we are God's children, and what we will be has not yet appeared, but we know that when He appears we shall be like Him, because we shall see Him as He is"* (1 John 3:2). When John says we shall be "like Him," it does not mean that we will have taken on the nature of God. We will always be created beings, totally dependent upon His life for our existence. But we will be "like Him" in the sense that we share more and more in His holiness, purity and joy.

All of this is, of course, a great mystery. But, if we look at this world and see what God did in "six days with a handful of dust," we can hardly imagine what He has fashioned for all eternity. I don't know about you, but I can hardly wait!

> *I believe that we will rise with bodies new forevermore;*
> *Living in a New Creation with the God whom we adore.*

Apostles' Creed Hymn

When singing the *Apostles' Creed Hymn* as a unified whole, other tunes besides *Stuttgart* may be used by combining two stanzas together at a time. Possible tunes include: *Beecher* (Love Divine, All Loves Excelling), *Ode to Joy* (Joyful, Joyful, We Adore Thee) or *Austrian Hymn* (Glorious Things of Thee are Spoken).

Apostles' Creed Hymn

HYMN TUNE: STUTTGART
WORDS BY JULIE TENNENT

1

I believe in God the Father,
mighty yet the fount of love;

Maker of the whole creation,
earth below and heav'n above.

2

I believe in Jesus Christ,
His only Son before all time;

All authority is His,
our Lord and Savior, Word divine.

3

He stepped into time and hist'ry,
by the Spirit was conceived;

Born in flesh of Virgin Mary,
humble servant who believed.

4

Jesus suffered under Pilate,
and was cruelly crucified;

Entered death which was our sentence,
ours the sin for which He died.

5

*To the dead He then descended, entering to
claim His own;*

*Leading forth a host of captives, casting
Satan from his throne.*

6

*On the third day Christ arose, triumphant
over death's domain;*

*Firstfruit of the New Creation,
victor over Satan's reign.*

7

*He ascended into Heaven,
seated at the Father's hand;*

*For our lives He's interceding
till on earth He takes His stand.*

8

*Jesus Christ will come again
to judge the living and the dead;*

*Then the world will be made right with
Jesus as our living head.*

9

*I believe the Triune God
is Father, Holy Spirit, Son;*

*I believe the Holy Spirit
is with them forever one.*

10

*I believe there is one holy Church
for whom Christ bled and died;*

*Saints throughout the world and time who
share communion as His bride.*

11

*Wondrous gift of sins' forgiveness,
purchased at a costly price;*

*Freely must be giv'n to others, honoring
Christ's sacrifice.*

12

*I believe that we will rise
with bodies new forevermore;*

*Living in a New Creation
with the God whom we adore.*

About the Author

Dr. Timothy Tennent received his M.Div. in 1984 from Gordon-Conwell; the Th.M. in Ecumenics, with a focus on Islam from Princeton Theological Seminary; and did graduate work in linguistics (TESL) at the University of Georgia. He completed his Ph.D. in Non-western Christianity with a focus on Hinduism and Indian Christianity in 1998 at the University of Edinburgh in Scotland. He served eleven years as professor of World Missions and Indian Studies at Gordon-Conwell Theological Seminary in South Hamilton, Massachusetts. He has ministered and taught in China, Thailand, Nigeria, Eastern Europe, and India. Ordained in the United Methodist Church, he has pastored churches in Georgia, and preached regularly in churches throughout New England and across the country.

In 2009, Dr. Tennent was inaugurated as the eighth president of Asbury Theological Seminary. In addition to his service as president of the Seminary and professor of World Christianity, he is author to a growing collection of books and publications on missions and global Christianity. He also serves on the faculty of Luther W. New Jr. Theological College of Dehra Dun, India where he has taught annually since 1989.

Visit TimothyTennent.com to follow Dr. Tennent's blog,
listen to his sermons, and further connect with his work.
Follow him on Twitter @timtennent.

CPSIA information can be obtained
www.ICGtesting.com
ted in the USA
W020931260720
5LV00002B/2